Along the Way

Footprints from a Long Journey

Priscilla Gifford

Enjoy!

Priscilla Gifford

Along the Way

Copyright © 2018 by Priscilla Gifford

ISBN-13 : 978-1723226977

Dedicated to my family and friends

Acknowledgments

Anne Gifford (Cover art, technical and emotional support)

Golden West Writing Group (Opportunity)

Linda Holbrook (Photography)

Terra Rafael (This book's caring midwife)

Rick Shepard (Computer wizardry)

Jyoti Wind (Quiet encouragement)

Table of Contents

RANDOMLY

Once Upon a Time

Listen to the wisps of our childhood:

A merry girl skipping through the woods to a big surprise at grandma's house.
The captive princess' golden tresses cascading from the tower.
The trail of bread crumbs on the forest path.
Evil queens, poisoned apples, talking mirrors and long, long sleeps.
Darkly looming forests and kind woodsmen.
Straw being spun into gold, a clever girl and an enraged captor.
Cruel stepsisters, transformed pumpkins and glass slipper salvation.
Nocturnal cobbler elves.
A shunned duckling.
A blond girl OCD intruder in a bears' cottage.
Goats and trolls and bridges.
One hysterical doom-saying small hen.
Three pigs comparing the strength of building materials.
Porridge, blackbird pie and curds and whey.
Jungle pancakes with tiger butter.
Wolves of every ilk: huffing and puffing, cross-dressing, ever lurking, always evil.
Princes—brave handsome magical heirs, seeking beauty and justice on white horses.
Fairy godmothers with wands and conditions to be met.

Were we frightened? Were we taught moral lessons? Were we enchanted?

Yes, no, maybe.

Somehow, we survived it all.
Some of us even may have lived happily ever after.

Some of us may still become white swans.

Every Day is a Beginning

To wake up
To get up
To get dressed
To get out
To be surprised
To give thanks.

Breathing

The woman pants, takes deep breaths and pushes.
Then, the baby slips into the world, breathes and cries.
The mother inhales the sweetness of her baby's skin.

The child, learning to swim, patterns her breathing
And soon is crawling across the water's surface.

The kids challenge each other to breath-holding contests,
Straining until their faces turn maroon and their chests ache,
Until they stop, one by one, saved by a heaving gasp.

We breathe, absorbing lilacs, new-cut grass, damp spring earth,
Bread in the oven, chili sauce in the kettle,
Sheets fresh from the clothesline,
Pungent salve on our feverish chests,
Father's aromatic pipe,
Mother's hand lotion as she strokes our cheek--
The soothing aromas of home.

We breathe together as our bodies join in love.
We sigh as we surface to life, afterward.

And, at the end, there is a final farewell breath,
A last period to it all.

We who are left are told to take deep breaths to ease our grief,
To clear our thoughts, to still our minds.

What a natural sweet remedy.
Breathing is something we all know how to do.

My House

I have lived in my house for almost ninety years, and there
have been many changes.

When I moved in, it was small and required a lot of attention
from my doting parents. The plumbing system was particularly
undependable, but corrected itself in about two years with
much patient training.

Through the years, the house expanded to meet my growing
needs. After about eighteen years, all systems were working
well. The exterior and trim changed in large and small ways
and even developed a modest curb appeal.

The house remained sturdy and resilient until it reached forty,
when the heating system became totally unreliable. The ther-
mostat was completely out of adjustment. Everything would
be comfortable until disturbed by a sudden burst of heat so
warm that it caused a temporary reddening of the exterior and
condensation. These were difficult years, but soon comfort
was restored.

I remodeled as necessary, removing once reliable parts of the
various mechanical systems. Some needed only a simple repair.
As the years went by, more maintenance was needed and
professional advice was sought to solve problems. The exterior
and trim gradually lost its original smooth finish, and, after
some initial attempts to restore it, I decided to settle for basic
care appropriate for its advancing age.

My house has served me faithfully through all these years, and
I will continue to appreciate it and treat it well. However, the
day will come when I will have to move out. I have made
plans to have parts of it recycled, and the rest composted.
My next dwelling? I'll see.

Why Do I Write?

Many reasons.

Because I love words—the sounds, the meanings, the origins, the searching for and finding just the right one to express an idea.

Because I can express an emotion that otherwise might lie buried---the joy would be stifled, the grief hidden. By writing about my feelings, I am able to better work through them.

Because I can give shape and form to memory, and, in sifting through the layers of my mind, relive those events that have made me "me". In so doing, I leave a record for my family.

Because it is a way to reach out to others, by sending birthday blessings, notes of appreciation, messages of comfort in dark times, or simply saying , "Hello, my friend!"

Because it allows me to organize my thoughts and express an opinion.

Because it allows me to use my experience in writing to spread information to others and to be useful.

Because, finally, it is fun, and it is free.

Musings on Music

A miraculous mystery.
A mysterious miracle.

The composer in his garret, many, many years ago,
Hears a melody deep in his mind, his heart, his soul.
He sits at his harpsichord, and finds the keys
That bring the tune to life.

With quill pen and ink, he draws lines on precious paper,
And the melody becomes black dots, some with flags, some
plain,
Hundreds of them dancing on the lines, each one a key to be
pressed,
Moving forward rhythmically, regularly measured,
Flowing in mathematical beauty--- creative thought made
tangible.

And the wonder is that today, we can sit at a piano,
Open a copy of that music and follow those markings,
Playing his melody just as he dreamed it long ago.
Just as thousands have done,
Just as the music will echo and delight as long as people
Read the dots and claim the gift.

A mysterious miracle.
A miraculous mystery.

Compassion

The cross reaches in two directions:
One shaft guides our thoughts upward,
Seeking the Source of strength and understanding.
The arms stretch wide on each side,
Urging us to channel that love out to others.

We say, "Our hearts go out to them",
But our hands must follow.

December Light

In the deep dark of the year
As daylight dwindled
And blackness enveloped the long nights,
They sought the comfort of light.

Some danced in the wood
As sparks from their brave fires
Sputtered up into the unknown.

Some found surprising oil,
Saving a temple and a people.

Some saw a dazzling star
Leading to a child, and hope.

Today, December is still bleak.
New darknesses press around us
And we yearn, we yearn for light.

The eight candles still burn.
The bright star shines on.

We need only to look, and to see.

Kaleidoscope

Simple beauty.
Magical mirrors and colored glass.
Dazzling patterns,
Each rotation revealing a unique design---
"Ooh, look! Ah, see this one!"
Then, a quick twist, and the pattern mutates,
The new one different, still brilliant, intricate.
Jewel-like beauty.

But, still only a device of glass and mirrors
Until we hold it to the light---
Light, the ingredient that creates the artful alchemy,
The joyful geometry.

Light has the possibility to transform
If we will only turn toward it.

Stained Glass

The pale plaster walls of the old church
Stand glorified on each side
By large stained glass windows.

A kneeling woman by the empty tomb,
Unaware of the angels and the risen One nearby;
The Boy preaching to skeptical robed elders;
Jewel colors cut and artfully leaded
To channel the brilliant sun inside,
Painting the quiet space
With riches of light.

As the sunlight sets windows aglow,
So a smile from a friend
Brightens a waiting heart.

Where Two or Three Are Gathered

A cool summer evening, sun just gone,
Mountains darkening against the gold-streaked sky.
Friends join hands in a solemn circle,
Gathered to strengthen a family plunged into deep waters.

We read a universal prayer together.
Then, wrapped in haunting primitive music,
Each one sends silent prayers and thoughts and love,
Launching the energy out to where hope and healing dwell.

The music ends.

Our eyes lift to a sliver of moon.

September 11, 2001

A shocked people, fixed on the television screen,
Where, over and over, the planes crashed,
The towers crumbled into ash.
The frantic ones ran, looking over their shoulders
At the stifling gray cloud behind them.

We watched, again and again,
As if hoping that, maybe this time,
No one would jump to certain death,
The towers would still gleam, unscarred,
And somehow, it would all go away.

The next day, wanting to help, we stood in long lines
To donate blood that would not, in the end, be needed.
This was a different kind of disaster;
A pulverized body needs no transfusion.

Churches opened at midnight for prayer.
We clung together, united in our shared frightened grief.

Our leaders asked very little of us.
They told us to go on with our lives,
To absorb the blow bravely. That was it.

Then, out came the flags from the garages and attics
Where they had been resting since the Fourth of July.
Streets in small towns and cities were lined with red, white and
blue.
Banners flew from front porches, tall buildings, lightposts,
bridges, cars, trucks, bicycles.

Old Glory burst forth on tee-shirts, hats and lapel pins.
Local merchants sold out their red, white and blue stock.

We were awash in patriotism.
Our flags were our small strong gesture, something to do,
A simple symbol to get us through whatever was to come.

After Paris

My mind stumbles out of sleep into November sun.
The Paris terror with which I went to bed surfaces again.
The radio spells out the fearsome facts---bombs, horror,
hatred, death.
Despair surrounds me with "Why?"

Then, there on the wall, a small, perfect rainbow;
The glass prism on the windowsill casts its familiar span of
colors.

Eternal order remaining within our chaos.

Inauguration 2017

We tense, as it starts,
Not knowing where we are led,
Praying for our land.

Will the Dream end here?
Union bruised by fear and hate.
Can we be the salve?

Summer 2018

Hearts and minds are pierced.
Each day, new insults wound us.
Will the center hold?

Our fabric unravels.
Compassion, justice are torn.
Can our vote mend us?

Oasis

As we journey through the hills and valleys of our lives,
As we struggle across the dry desert stretches,
We yearn for an oasis.
A berth of cool comfort
With water for our parched souls,
With shade for our weary minds.
An oasis where we can be restored, revived and refreshed to travel on.

Our church can be that haven in our troubled world.
There, together, we may just possibly find calm and rest and strength
In this hurting, battered world, so thirsty for peace and love.

Worldwide Communion Day

Together, again
To do this - - - the loaf, the cup - - -
Remembering the Gift.

On the Cruise

We cruise North,
The ship so huge we may just lose our way to meals and sleep.

From the deck, we watch the massive ice wall crack and crumble.
We point from the rail as two whales swim, not too close.
They fix us with their cold stares.

 Do the whales, as we who watch them, have the thought,
"How strange—these small creatures, so unlike us.
 But see, their eyes show signs of life and sense."

If God made both us and the whales, who can say which has more worth,
When each is tuned to live its own life plan?

After

Day after Easter:
Laundry, bills, television.
Egg salad sandwich.

At Stonehenge

We stood among them,
Dwarfed by their dark silent strength,
Awed by the ages.

Clearing

Rains gone, sun returns.
Tamped-down hearts stir and are warmed,
Enkindled by light.

The Movie in the Closet

Our Writing Group was gathered in our senior community's meeting room, ready to share our monthly offerings. But, the room was not quiet---low voices were coming from the closet, where the equipment for the afternoon's in-house movie was housed. We proceeded over the soundtrack, which was not too intrusive, but always there.

Later, I thought about it. Perhaps, in our lives, there is always a movie playing in the closet.

We go on about our daily business, but each of us has concerns hovering back there in our minds. Maybe financial worries. Perhaps a prickly personal relationship. A child's school experience. A puzzling or chronic health situation. Aging. Looming property decisions. Depression. Issues about the environment and the state of the world. A sub-text of unease.

We keep on, day by day, with the shut-away movie running along, always there.

PERSONALLY

Multiple Me

Who am I?

Daughter: A much-loved, long-awaited only child, spoiled and encouraged, quiet, conscientious, studious.

Granddaughter: Surrounded by love from my red-haired Irish "Nanny" (seamstress, baker, ever my defender), and my tidy little Dutch grandma (farm wife, Bible reader, gentle soul).

Cousin: Childhood summer visits to the farm, playing with my surrogate siblings in the barn, eating warm ripe tomatoes in the field with the juice running down our chins, croquet and Parcheesi.

Girlfriend: Somehow, connecting with a few boys to take me to high school dances, movies, picnics, football games--- walking everywhere. Later on, college dates--lots of conversation and coffee.

Wife and Lover: Young, learning to balance needs, the check-book and lives with laughs, a few sparks and tears but, always, love.

In-Law: Finding a strong, patient other mother who always wanted the best for our growing family. Adding a quirky brother and a sister with whom to share the peaks and valleys.

Aunt: Watching three young people move along on their special paths.

Mother: Beyond the diapers, the braces, measles and misunderstandings, lengthened skirts and patched jeans, school plays, projects and graduations, there was pride, wonder and love for these two unique souls who were given to us.

Mother-in-Law: Welcoming my children's partners into our small family fold, accepting them and their gifts with affection.

Friend: Sharing laughs, tears and the ordinary and miraculous with golden companions all along the way.

Widow: Alone again after only 25 years, keeping busy with work, my church family, antique collecting and selling, village causes, my also-hurting children. Going on, remembering the love.

Grandmother: Finally, welcoming someone new to care for, to weep and smile over, to nourish, and to teach me to be a child again.

Naming the Baby

Parents-to-be, finally after many years,
Searching their thrilled brains for a name for the baby.
"Barbara" or "Peter", they had decided.

Then, spending a summer day at the county fair,
Hearing a mother call to a little red-haired girl,
"Priscilla, Priscilla Anne".
In an instant, the couple smiled at each other and knew.
"That's the name if we have a girl."

A few months later, I entered their loving world,
And my hair was red.

A Memory - Age 4

I cuddle on the sofa (we called it a davenport), close to my
mother,
Dark blue plush cushions prickling my bare legs.
Together, we turn the pages of my favorite thick story book
Where Jocko the Monkey has circus fun.

My mother's sea green wool dress is soft.
A row of small round gold buttons marches up each sleeve,
Each one with a small cloth loop.
How many times did I unfasten and fasten those loops
As my mother patiently tried to continue the story?

Enough times for me to feel warm and loved, even today.

Siblings

We were almost her siblings.
She was four when we slipped out--- not yet ready.
Too early to breathe, too soon even to cry.
Quickly, the two of us, here and gone.

She grew up alone, fiercely loved,

Never knowing we had almost been there.
No sharing of bedrooms and angel food cake.
No passing down the dresses that grandma sewed.
No tugging over toys, no scrambling for lap time.
No giggling together under the covers.
No Parcheesi and popcorn.
No smiling family photos.
No nieces or nephews.

She never knew about us.

Much later, she learned of us by chance,
Only a few words from a friend, nothing more.
We remained hidden in our parents' remembering hearts.

Now, years gone by, our sister remains an only, lonely child,
Wishing we had grown and cried and loved together,
Wanting to review her life with someone who had shared all
the years.

Yearning to meet us, at last.

Privilege

Looking back at my early years, I realize I was privileged.
I had a dad who took me fishing, bought books for me, went
to church with me every Sunday, taught me to play checkers
and poker and Monopoly and shine my shoes. He made
Shirley Temples for me when the adults were drinking high-
balls. He bought me a harmonica so we could play together as
we drove on country roads. He took me to adventure and
historical movies. We colored Easter eggs. He shared his
wonder at sunsets and Northern lights. He was proud of his
Navy service. He supported us, somehow, during the Depression.
I had a mom who cooked good meals and catered to my food
fussiness, who drilled me with endless words when I entered
spelling bees, who taught me how to iron handkerchiefs and
dish towels, and how to darn a sock. She showed me how to
make my bed, telling me, "Make a fine bed, have a fine husband", which I would later understand. She saw that I took
dancing lessons, although I never made it to a recital. She
worked in a department store and used her employee's dis-
count to keep me in plaid skirts and soft sweaters and saddle
shoes. She taught me pride in my appearance. She showed me
how to make fudge and stuffed dates, and braided my hair and
sent me off to Girl Scout camp.
My maternal grandmother lived with us, and baked angel food
cakes from scratch, hand-beating a dozen eggs, and made
fragrant molasses cookies. A professional seamstress, she
taught me how to hem a dishtowel, and make a doll's yo-yo
quilt of puckered cotton circles, and later, how to use her old
treadle sewing machine. She made sweet dresses. She read
stories to me, and took me to the evening hymn sing at her

Baptist church, where we sang songs much livelier than the Presbyterian's. She made popcorn and cocoa when we were alone when my folks were out for the evening, and we played Old Maid. She spoiled me.

My paternal grandmother welcomed me for two weeks each summer to her farm home, where she cooked and fussed over me, and read me Bible stories. She told me about coming to the United States from Holland with her family when she was only sixteen, and being employed and mentored by an upstate New York Dutch family. She showed me how to fluff up a feather bed so that it rose smooth and plump. When we picked cherries, she worked next to me and helped fill my pail, for which I was paid two cents a pound. She took me to her Dutch Reformed Church, where the sermon was in her native language but the message was true. Every Christmas, she gave me Dutch brown sugar and vinegar candy and a pair of hand knit mittens.

I was privileged, not with wealth, family position, prestige or social status.

I was privileged because I was simply loved.

Pals

My dad and I were pals. I was a skinny red-haired only child,
He called me Squirt.

When he didn't have the price of a ticket to the circus,
We went to the railroad yard before dawn
And saw the elephants and camels being led off the brightly-
painted cars.

In early spring, he sought out pussy willow bushes.
We scrambled down a muddy stream bank, me in my red
rubber boots,
To gather a furry bouquet.

He taught me how to fish:
To pierce the wriggling worm with the barbed hook
To sense the fish's nibble and when to yank and set the hook
To reel in the flopping perch, and, later, bass and lake trout
To sit patiently in the rented wooden boat, sun glaring down
on the lake
And finally to chug toward shore, listening to the old
Evinrude.

He helped me learn how to swim.
He inflated my tan cotton water wings and stood in the shal-
low lake,
Urging me on as I lay on them and paddled around,
Finally applauding my first strokes on my own.

He taught me how to play checkers on winter evenings,
Showing me no mercy until I learned to win fair and square.

He was a reader, slouched in his easy chair, smoking his pipe:
The Saturday Evening Post, Life, Liberty, American Legion
magazine.
Adventure novels from the rental library.
He bought me books. I read, following his example.

He loved to tell jokes, and I learned to laugh.

He taught me to play poker: five-card stud, straight draw, spit-
in-the-ocean.
Stacks of red, white and blue chips and peanuts on the table.

He was a restaurant equipment salesman.
On Saturdays, while my mother sold dresses in the department
store,
I tagged along with him on business calls.
Sitting in an empty tavern at a small Formica table,
Last night's beer still pungent in the air, the neon backbar
signs sputtering.
I sipped ginger ale and read a Big Little Book,
Waiting for him to sell four dozen beer glasses.
Then, another sales stop at a diner.
I always had an egg and olive sandwich and a chocolate malted
milk shake.

He showed me how to polish my only pair of brown school
shoes,
Putting newspaper on the kitchen table as we daubed and
buffed to keep up appearances.

On Sundays, we walked to church and Sunday school
While my mom usually stayed home cooking a pot roast..

I rode beside him on the prickly plush seat of his '34 Dodge.
No radio, but we had music.
He sang songs from World War I, popular songs, hymns. I
learned them all.
Sometimes we'd pull our harmonicas out of the glove com-
partment and cruise along, he steering with one hand, playing
and singing.

He showed me, in these ordinary ways, how good a child's life
could be.
He provided.

I don't remember his ever saying, "I love you".
But I knew, I knew.

Starry, Starry Night

When I was eleven, my parents managed to send me to Girl Scout camp for a week. We lived in tents on the shore of Owasco Lake, one of the central New York State Finger Lakes. Our time was filled with crafts, games, swimming, boating, nature hikes and evening campfires with songs and stories. It was an enriching week for this only child.

A highlight was a canoe trip across the narrow lake, cooking supper on the beach and making s'mores. Far away from any artificial light, the night sky was black, but absolutely filled with stars. The counselors pointed out the Big Dipper and the Milky Way and other constellations, we sang "Taps" (Day is done, gone the sun, from the lake, from the hills, from the sky. All is well, safely rest, God is nigh.) We called "Good night, Scouts" to each other.

Then, I settled into my sleeping bag on the gravel shore, and looked up at the endless sky. It must have been meteor shower season, because there were many shooting stars, and I watched them flame across the sky until the gentle lapping of the waves lulled me to sleep.

I have always remembered that magical night.

Indeed, God was nigh.

Priscilla

There was a young girl named Priscilla,
Who met a mild man from Manila.
He was lacking in zest,
And she wanted the best:
Pistachio, not merely vanilla.

My Vicarious Pleasure

Here come the Winter Olympics and along with them, the figure skating competition. We'll watch hours of lithe young athletes gliding and spinning and jumping on perfect ice in their perfect costumes to perfect music. And I, in my chair in my flannel robe will be out there with them.

I could never really ice skate. Oh, I tried. My small city in upstate New York had many cold winters. The large pond at Hoopes Park, which was home to swans and surrounded by rose gardens in the summer, froze over in winter. On cold afternoons, I would hurry home from school, pick up the phone and call Whipple and Forman's, the old sporting goods store. If there was safe ice for skating, they hung a large red wooden ball from their outdoor sign. This was before the days of automated messages, so the store clerks must have spent a lot of time answering calls. If the ball was there, I called my friend, Joanie, and made plans to meet.

I changed into warm snow pants, jacket, hat, scarf and mittens, pulled on my boots and walked two blocks to catch the city bus to the park. My white shoe skates, with wool socks tucked inside, were slung over my shoulder. This was around 1938, the heyday of Sonja Henie, a perky blond Olympic champion turned movie queen, but no one in my town wore short skating skirts like hers.

At the park, I went into the wooden garden house, which had a stone fireplace at one end, a small snack bar (cocoa, soda- which we called "pop"- and candy bars), rest rooms, and wooden benches. Joanie and I found each other, sat down and

36

laced on our skates, put our shoes in open cubby holes and headed out to the rink.

Joanie was a good skater. I was not. Off she glided, finding many of our friends from school. Regularly, she circled back to where I wobbled around the edges of the ice on my weak ankles. I made trips to the garden house to sit by the fire; then, back out to the frigid embarrassment.

Around five as it grew dark, we would take off our skates and head home on the bus to a warm dinner, and an evening of listening to the radio. Fibber McGee and Molly, Mr. Keene-Tracer of Lost Persons, Jack Armstrong, I Love a Mystery, Edgar Bergen and Charlie McCarthy, and the Quiz Kids were favorite programs. I don't remember much homework.

Starting in fifth grade, this went on for several years. My pals were patient. I never improved. I don't think my parents ever came to watch - - -a blessing all around. They assumed that we hundred or so kids were safe at the city park, and there must have been some supervision to prevent the older boys on their black hockey skates from terrorizing the rest of us. I gave up finally when I outgrew my skates.

But now, every four years I flop down in my recliner in front of the television, cozy and warm, and glide around the glistening ice on strong ankles. No chapped lips, no dripping nose, no numb toes - - - just me and the music. And maybe a cup of cocoa.

Dancing Class

Dance class spring party.
Age ten, cautious slow fox trot.
Pink punch and moist palms.

First Date

A movie; we walk.
Ice cream on the way back home.
Kiss? Maybe next time.

Music

Stardust

When I hear that song,
We're dancing, out by the lake,
Glitter ball sparkling.

Song Remembered

Warm, pure melody
Enfolding me in a cloak
Of softest velvet.

Independence Day

Each of us has had independence days.

The day we gave up our mother's comforting always-warm breast.

The day we toddled alone for the first time after weeks of wobbling around hanging onto furniture and our parents' hands.

The day we proudly gave up diapers after many attempts at the control that meant so much to our mother.

The day we first walked all the way to school alone after our mom had walked with us until we learned the way safely.

The day we sat down and read a book by ourselves.

The wonderful day when we at last learned to balance on our two-wheel bike and ride without mom or dad running along beside to steady us. Freedom!

The day we were allowed to go to the movies with friends instead of our parents.

The night our parents felt we were old enough to be left alone, nervously with all the lights turned on, in the evening while they went to the movies.

The day our parents permitted us to go on a date, watching as we stepped out the door with tremulous excitement and nervousness.

The day we got our operator's license and were allowed to drive the family car—alone.

The day we graduated from high school, leaving behind twelve years of friends and familiar surroundings, moving on.

Perhaps every day is an independence day, separating us from that which has been, carrying us to that which will be. All those little steps leading us to now.

Unpredictable

His orbit in life was not a predictable concentric circle.
His path was wonderfully skewed, elliptical.
I stood in the middle, a self-appointed anchor to normality
While he swirled around out there - - -
Sometimes stressed, or carelessly optimistic, or happily goofy.
But ah, when he orbited closer to my stolid center,
The beauty of his eccentricity
Leaped across the open space to inflame our hearts.

Our First Creche

It was December, 1950. My husband, Paul, and I, married in June, were preparing to celebrate our first Christmas in our rented house in Hamburg, Pennsylvania. We were on an extremely limited budget. I think some friends gave us a real tree, and others gave us some lights and ornaments they no longer needed. I made some popcorn and strung it to drape on the branches. We put a white pillowcase around the base of the tree.

Now, all we needed was a stable and figures to put under the tree. Woolworth's would surely have just what we needed. This was before the time of Wal-Mart and Target; almost every town in the country had a small "Five and Dime" where you could find cosmetics, mops, greeting cards, oilcloth for the kitchen table, live pet birds and goldfish, sheet music, toys and almost everything in between.

So, off we went. We were thrilled to find a small wooden stable and the Christmas story figures to go in it. Some statuettes were only ten cents, while the heavier donkey and camel were fifteen cents. We bought Mary, Joseph, baby Jesus in a cardboard manger, three wise men, two shepherds, and a few sheep. When we arranged the ensemble under the tree, we felt our Christmas was complete. There was even a hole in the back of the stable for a light to shine on the holy scene.

Well, I still use that creche. We later added a cow, made in Germany, that had been mine as a child, and a few more sheep. The plaster figures, never finely molded or painted, show sixty-eight years of wear—being packed in tissue paper, moving twelve times, and being arranged by our children's small hands. There was never any discussion of upgrading— this is the Gifford family "manger", as we call it. I still set it up on the first Sunday of Advent.

Over the years, I have gathered a collection of small nativity scenes from around the world, made of straw, wood, pottery, and quartz. None is as beautiful to me as our first set, for that is surrounded by memory and love.

The China Clock

This is the story of one of my treasured possessions, an old
china clock. It came to us in 1950 when my husband and I,
newly-married, set up housekeeping in Hamburg, Pennsylvania. Across the street lived Mr. Fink, an older Pennsylvania
Dutch man who had an antique shop in his home. There we
found the lovely clock. It had a pale blue and white case,
delicately painted with flowers and gold scrolls, and was
marked Bonn China, Germany. We decided to buy it for my
mother-in-law's Christmas gift, but the price was $30, a large
sum for a couple with a combined yearly income of $2500. Mr.
Fink let us pay $5.00 a month for six months, and the clock
had a new home.

Grandma Gifford was surprised and thrilled with the gift,
which was placed on a lace doily on her desk, its gentle chime
marking the hours. When poor health forced her to sell her
home, the clock moved with her to her sunny corner room at
her daughter's big square farmhouse. When she died, one year
after her son's passing, my dear sister-in-law presented the
clock to me. It had a place of honor on my desk. Over the
years, it received a new face to replace the discolored original,
and had periodic cleanings and tune-ups.

When, in turn, I gave up my home and moved to Boulder, we
packed the clock carefully and placed it in the car for the big
move West, not trusting this treasure to the movers. However,
four-hundred miles into the trip, near Cleveland, we had an
accident on a rain-slick road and totaled the car. Perhaps
miraculously, the china clock survived.

We continued our trip by plane, swaddlng the clock carefully in bubble wrap and tucking it into my carry-on suitcase. It survived two security inspections, and finally arrived safely at my new senior community.

As I write this, its rhythmic tick and soft chime keep me company, noting the hours with sweet memories.

Ghost Story - 1953

We lived in a stone cottage, the former gatehouse to the
historic Robert Livingston estate on the Hudson River in New
York State. For 50 years it had been the home of the estate's
caretaker and his wife, the manor's housekeeper. After they
died, the Livingstons updated the old house with fresh paint
and wallpaper, and we were the first to rent it. We were thrilled
with the wide plank floors and country orchard setting.

When we moved in, an upright pump parlor organ remained in
an upstairs bedroom, left behind for a few weeks. We were
told that it had stood in the living room, where the former lady
of the house had played it often.

I was happily several months pregnant with our first child. My
husband was in charge of the laboratory in a small community
hospital, and was often called out at night on emergencies.

On one such evening, I was lying on our living room couch
reading, with our golden cocker spaniel, Tippy, at my side. The
dog's ears suddenly perked up and he raised his head. It was
then that I heard the organ music. It was not a melody, but
changing chords, swelling and fading, filling the air around us
with very definite sound. After several minutes, silence again.

I don't remember being frightened, but it definitely got my
attention. When my husband came home, I told him what had
happened.

He sat down next to me and said, "You, too?" He confessed
that he had heard the same music on nights when he lay on the

couch after I had gone upstairs to bed. He had never told me because he feared that I might be nervous about being alone in the isolated house.

We never heard those chords again. Perhaps it was only the wind in the chimney. I like to think they were a welcoming blessing to the young couple in the old stone housestead.

Birth Day

Floating in darkness,
Growing, waiting, warmed by love,
She slides Here, from There.

Lullaby

I sing "Sleep, My Child",
Wishing her love and safety - - -
A mother's deep dream.

Royalty and Us - May, 1954

The Duke and Duchess of Windsor were coming for tea, and we had to cut the grass. This is a true story. Let me explain.

We had rented the gatehouse of the Robert Livingston estate on the Hudson River in eastern New York. The original Chancellor Livingston had been Thomas Jefferson's Secretary of State. The current Livingston descendants, a reserved middle-aged couple, lived simply in the large old tan stone house. The Chancellor's delicate gold French chairs and settees stood in the parlor overlooking the river and the gentle hills beyond. The family raised apples, and, in the winter, went by train to their Manhattan apartment for the opera.

Back in the late 18th and early 19th centuries, this section of the river had been home to families of wealth and position, and was still lined with their estates.

The Duke and his Duchess, idling away their exiled abdicated years here and there away from the British Isles, were on a visit to the United States They were being feted that spring day by the Hudson River aristocracy, lunching at another estate further down the river.

Mrs. Livingston was entertaining everyone at tea. She called us a few days ahead to ask if we could see to it that our front lawn was mown by Saturday, as the entourage would be driving past the gatehouse. Naturally, we agreed. She was also anxious about her having time to freshen the powder room before everyone arrived. She had hired a local woman to help with the tea, and was, of course, nervous.

Well, we only had an old dull hand lawnmower which had been provided with the stone cottage rental. It may have been the first cutting of the season, a bit overdue and shaggy. My husband, Paul, was working overtime in the laboratory of a small hospital nearby. I had just that week weaned our eight-month-old baby, Anne, and my swollen tender breasts prevented me from pushing the mower.

Paul worked on the lawn until dark for two evenings until it was much tidier, but probably with room for more landscaping touches. He was not exactly a cheerful laborer. It was the best we could do. We later thought it would have been a generous gesture for the Livingstons to have sent over one of their hired men for the job, but they may have been grooming the big sloping lawn on the estate. Or perhaps lawn care was listed in our rental contract.

The great day arrived. We kept watch in the afternoon, and, finally, a procession of large expensive automobiles drove past, headed toward the river, moving rather more rapidly than I had visualized. I assume that the Duke and Duchess were in one of these cars.

They didn't wave.

Oh, Shirley

Shirley just loved to go dancing.
She burned up the floor with her prancing.
But when the band halted,
To the lawn Shirley vaulted
To squeeze in a bit of romancing.

Our Cats

Our cats were named Sugar and Spice,
And they simply did not care for mice.
They would much rather dine
On good cheeses and wine
Or a platter of salmon on ice.

A Very Particular Man

A very particular man
Would eat only those foods that were tan.
He avoided all greens
But ate navy beans
And mushrooms, right out of the can.

Poughkeepsie

There was an old man from Poughkeepsie
Who frequently drank until tipsy.
He staggered around
'Til he fell to the ground.
Now he lives in the woods like a gypsy.

The Fisherman

Saffron leaves, once summer's green canopy, drifted down, decorating the cold mountain stream and its browned banks. The clear water swirled gently around his dry feet, encased in waders. This autumn day was one of those gift days, suddenly mild after an early snowfall had ended the woods' season of growth. He had seized it for one last day of fishing for the season.

This was a familiar stream, a favorite. He selected a special fly, one that had proved tempting to these trout. His cast was precise, directed to a placid pool. The delicate filament glistened as it flashed through the brisk air. He played the line skillfully, hoping to get a fish's attention but no strike. He kept on, each cast crafted by years of practice. He would stay on, moving along the bank, buoyed by the crisp fall air, warmed by the sun, more direct now that the trees were baring their branches

It didn't really matter if a fish rose to the skittering fly. It was enough to simply be there, quietly alone, for one more day.

A Lake Memory

An October bonus day.
Shirt-sleeve warm.
The long deep lake lies calm
Among the sloping hills and vineyards
Aflame with autumn.

We're with my father in his 12-foot boat.
My little girl and I.
He has steered us to this anchored spot to fish.

Growing up, hundreds of hours on this lake with him.
The tackle box, poles, tin minnow bucket, worms in the bait
can,
Smell of gasoline and warm baloney sandwiches.
Easy talk, sun-burned patience, waiting for a bite.
And now this perfect day, and someone young to teach.

I did not know this trip would be our last.
The moment lives, as he goes on before.

Our Ludwig

Our daughter, Anne, discovered Beethoven in a library book when she was nine, and was instantly enamored. She listened to symphony recordings, but wanted more, so she devised a costume. Her belted lavender bathrobe became a jacket. Her long pants were tucked into white knee socks for a bloused effect. Her brown oxford shoes were decorated with gold-painted cardboard buckles. One of her brother's long Tinker Toy rods served as a baton. She pulled her blond hair back in a ponytail and, voila, she was Ludwig. Whether sitting at our electronic organ or playing with the cat, she was happily transformed.

Sitting on the organ we had a small faux bronze bust of Beethoven, which was festooned with a paper hat on his birthday, December 16. A cake was also enjoyed, involving the family in this interlude.

Now, fast forward about thirty years. Anne's son, Lexis, age two, was playing in the den with his two grandmas, who were watching a television broadcast of the New York Philharmonic. He stopped playing with his cars, and stood in front of the TV. He immediately began mimicking Bernstein's conducting motions. We handed him a pencil for a baton, and he continued seriously for several minutes. His grandmas and parents were very happy.

Through the years, classical music has continued to echo in our homes. The bust sports his paper hat. Lex prefers Rachmaninoff.

Dream Machine

I was down in bed with the flu - - - the old-fashioned throbbing head, aching eyeballs, dripping nose, feverish body influenza. I had been blind-sided at work; I came home took two aspirin and crawled shivering into bed for almost a week.

Family life sputtered along. They ate canned soup, charred hot dogs, cinnamon toast and cocoa, graham crackers and applesauce, peanut butter and jelly, Frootloops---who knows what? I think it was before the days of pizza delivery. I must have forced ginger ale and eaten something. I mumbled directions and they tiptoed out away from the contagious room and left me alone.

I was lost in my dreams. One of the known symptoms of true influenza is feverish intense dreaming. It was like a movie that was running continuously with immediate seating. I could barely stay awake, drawn down into a bizarre but not frightening story.

I would drag my unkempt self to the bathroom, perhaps wash my face or brush my furry teeth and then plunge back to bed and the dream. Immediately, I was in the mesmerizing action of another world just waiting for me to close my eyes. As I recovered, the dream action faded away, my body grew stronger, I took a shower and picked up the pieces of my real mom life.

My theory is that the influenza dreams are a magical medicine, sent to lure the patient into the long hours of sleep that are necessary to recover.

This fits in with my theory that the reason pregnant women have to get up so many times during the night to use the bathroom is that it prepares them for their fragmented sleep after the baby is born.

I don't remember the fevered feature storyline, but it was a happy ending.

Patience

You promised to call.
My evening vanished, waiting.
Hours, patience --- both gone.

* * *

Whipping the egg whites,
Beater turning, wrist tiring---
Then, shiny meringue.

* * *

Yank the cord again.
The old motor finally starts.
Time to cut the grass.

* * *

He waits in the car.
"I'll be out in a minute".
He grins, toots the horn.

Getting Up in the Morning

This child had no problem with getting out of bed. Philip, a red-haired almost two-year-old, lived with his older brother, their parents and Rusty, the Irish setter, in a new country home. He slept in a crib in his own toy-filled room. The problem was that Philip had recently begun to awaken very early in the morning, before his brother, before his parents in their rooms down the hall. He was quiet - - - no crying or noise of any kind. He simply crawled over the side rail of the crib, slithered onto a nearby chair, left his room and got busy.

One morning he took a can of Comet cleanser from the cupboard under the kitchen sink, dragged a stool over and emptied the white powder all over the sink, the stove and everything else within the radius of his small but mighty arms, including the dog who had come to the kitchen, anticipating food.

That night, his parents moved his crib to the center of the room, confident that Philip would thus not be able to escape.

The very next morning, they heard Rusty running around and making happy sounds.

They found Philip curled up on the new white sofa, sharing chocolate cake with the slobbering grateful dog. The couch was well-festooned with chocolate frosting.

So, that night, they hung a bell on the door to their inventive toddler's room, hoping that would alert them to his early morning adventures.

Morning dawned on an empty crib. His mother had left her ironing board set up in the dining room, with the electric iron plugged in but turned off. Philip had pulled the iron, which landed sole down, on the new hardwood floor, and then turned it on. Luckily, he was not burned nor did he start a fire. There was only a black scorched triangle across two shiny board widths.

That night, the desperate parents lovingly tucked their busy boy into his crib and gave him his teddy bear. After he was angelically asleep, they fastened a badminton net securely over the top of the crib, tying it underneath. Hopefully, Philip would be caged.

The next morning, all was quiet. No clatter in the kitchen, no chocolate-begging dog, no smell of singed wood. Everyone slept peacefully. Dad was late for work, brother missed the school bus, and mother was very happy.

Superstitions

We search the night sky.
Look, there, a bright falling star.
Did you make a wish?

Kids comb through the grass,
Searching out four-leafed clovers.
Fresh good luck, no charge.

Thank you, kind bunny,
For giving up your hind foot
To bring me good luck.

Think of all the kids
Skipping over sidewalk cracks.
Lucky moms, pain free.

Magic

He was 9 years old with a new Presto Magic Kit.
There was a wooden magic wand,
A set of metal rings to connect or separate at will,
A deck of playing cards with many possibilities for bafflement,
A red silk scarf to pull from a sleeve or a small plastic tube,
A sliding cardboard box with its disappearing coin,
And, of course, a fully-illustrated instruction booklet,
Which promised our son entry into the world of wizardry.

He had placed all this mystical apparatus in a small brown leather case,
Originally a liquor case for the traveling man,
That had belonged to his grandpa,
It had a secure brass lock to preserve the age-old secrets.

The family sat patiently, dutifully amazed, as he performed.

A brief slice of a boy's life, and then,
ABRACADABRA - - - he was ten,
Ready to move on to other magic.

The Mysterious Woodpecker

Our family was gathered in the dining room for our evening meal, which we called "supper". We had only lived in our house for a month. A mature mountain ash tree with its clusters of orange berries stood in the narrow yard between us and our neighbors.

We talked as we ate, the usual everyday exchanges and silences of a boy, seven, a girl, ten and their two parents. Then, our meal was interrupted by a different sound coming in the open window: a series of rat-a-tats, a pause and then repeated clicks. The children hurried to the window looking for a woodpecker at work in the tree, but there was no bird. We went outside and peered up into the branches of the tree without success. What could it be?

This went on each evening for a week, but no bird was ever spotted. What could be making the noise? We were puzzled.

One afternoon I visited my next-door neighbor and found her and her husband seated at their kitchen table playing a game of Yahtzee, a game that uses five dice to score. They sat there, passing the cardboard tube back and forth, rattling the dice inside as they shook them and threw them on the table. I began to laugh—here was the phantom woodpecker. The sound of the shaken dice easily carried from their open kitchen window to our open dining room window next door, sounding very much like a determined woodpecker searching for insects.

They laughed when I explained. It was the end of a mystery, and the beginning of a wonderful friendship between neighbors.

Pokey

We lived in an upstate New York village of ten thousand, on a street with twenty houses and twenty-nine kids and, I think, four dogs. Pokey was one of the dogs, and he belonged to our neighbors, the Farleys.

The free-spirited family consisted of Dan, a gentle elementary school art teacher and Pied Piper to the street's children, his wife Jane, also a teacher but over-employed then as the mother of five little children, and Pokey.

Pokey was a rangy white hound of some sort, with a few brown splotches. He was good-natured and lively. There were no leash laws in the 1960's, and he roamed freely in the neighborhood, usually where children were playing. He tended to snatch whatever was loose and bring it home. Once or twice each winter, an apologetic Jane would appear at our back doors with a carton of scarves, single mittens, and knit hats, hoping to return them to their proper owners.

We shared a driveway with the Farleys, and one summer afternoon Pokey laruped home through the back yard, his teeth tightly gripping a large raw steak. The dog was followed closely by a red-faced man from the next street over, brandishing a long empty fork. Our son, Mark, was playing in the driveway.

"Is that your dog?" the man panted, wiping his face with his barbecue apron.

64

"No, he belongs next door," Mark answered, pointing quickly toward the Farley's house. Pokey had disappeared under his porch, happily chewing on the steak, safely out of reach. The Farleys were not at home, having piled earlier into their trusty old station wagon and driven away, leaving Pokey behind to his own devices.

The man pounded on the Farley's back door with no results. He asked Mark who lived there, and, after noting the family's name, stomped back through the yard to his empty charcoal grill and who knows how many picnickers, now destined to have a vegetarian feast. I am sure that the Farleys received a phone call when they came home, followed by meaty negotiations.

The Farleys later had prolific rabbits, but that is another story.

The Storm

It was a hot August afternoon, and I was alone in the house.
My folks and the baby had gone shopping for an hour. I was
eleven, and, as I heard the car leave the garage, I went to the
kitchen for a snack and a drink. Then I sprawled on the living
room couch for a nap. The house was quiet for a change, just
me alone.

I was dreaming peacefully when distant thunder awakened me.
Now, I have always been very frightened in thunderstorms---
afraid of the loud booms. Really terrified, I got off of the
couch and wandered around nervously, the noise coming
closer. I wished the folks would come home --- they always
made me feel safer.

What to do? I found a dark place to hide. I huddled, covered
my ears and endured the storm, shivering and very scared.
Thank goodness, it was a very brief storm. I was happy to hear
the folks come into the kitchen from the garage, calling my
name.

But, I was stuck in my hiding place, where they found me,
their pet cocker spaniel, Tippy, wedged under the old-
fashioned claw foot bathtub. In my thunder-panic, I had
managed to wiggle my way under the five-inch clearance, but
there I was wedged. I couldn't back out. I could only whimper.

Well, they had to lift the heavy iron bathtub a few inches off
the floor so I could scramble out backwards. I licked and
slobbered over their hands and danced around, grateful to be

free and moving again. Next time, I'll try to be more coura-
geous and just hide under a bed, a high bed.

Bruiser

Bruiser was a very large, very black, very hairy Newfoundland dog. He belonged to the McGraws, a lively family of six children and two harried parents who lived on our street. Bruiser was a well-known character in our village of 10,000.

Sometimes he just ambled out the front door, unnoticed. He was often tied to a large flagpole in the McGraw's front yard, but he was an escape expert. He then ranged the neighborhood and the village until someone called the family to come and get him. Other times, a kind friend with a large car would deliver him back home, his rope dangling from his collar.

One summer adventure led him to a neighbor's yard, where the tidy mother had just filled a new small inflatable swimming pool with water so her two daughters could frolic and cool off. Well, Bruiser beat them to it. We neighbors watched, trying not to smile too much, as Bruiser sat in the middle of the pool, shedding hair and other dog debris, water splashing over the sides, very little room to spare. The mother flailed away at him with her broom. Finally, one of the McGraw kids came to the rescue, and the dog jumped out and shook himself, a final baptism for the already wet and angry woman and everyone else within six feet of the, luckily, undamaged pool.

We became intimately involved with Bruiser when our female mutt, Spanky, went into heat. Bruiser camped out hopefully on our tiny back entry porch, making it very difficult to open our screen door. When Spanky needed to go out, one of us would put her on her leash and sneak out the front door, carrying a large stick. Motivated by his strong erotic instincts, Bruiser would bound around the house to meet us in front and immediately be at our side as we walked. We fended him off as he crowded us, drooling, his teeth chattering with frustrated passion. Well-aimed pokes with our stick kept the show moving until Spanky nervously did her business. We hurried back to the refuge of home. Bruiser followed and resumed his vigil on the back porch. We saw to it that Spanky never went into heat again.

And I Was Grateful

It was just a note in the mail
Written on a card with a flower on the front.

I saw her every day at work,
The usual easy talk at lunch.
But she knew, she knew what I needed
As the days inched into weeks,
As his body dwindled
And he began fading away
Into that place between here and There.

Just a note, a single line:
"A friend is thinking of you."

She knew.

Twenty-five

The hours of our lives drag or fly past---
Midnight to midnight, twenty-four hours, another day.
But what of those surprising times when, just for a moment,
We are suspended in a timeless twenty-five?

He's been away for months.
Life has crutched along, dragging your heart.
Now, he runs toward you from the plane.
Within his arms, love stops time—a twenty-five.

Not every time, but wonderfully often,
Our bodies are perfectly paced.
Together, slow and tender, then accelerating
To a breathless twenty-five.

The hours have inched along---
The timed pains, the purposeful breathing,
The stirrups, the ice chips, a grimaced final push;
Then, the slippery little being you will love forever---a miracu-
lous twenty-five.

Long bedside hours, watching his clock run down.
Listening to changing breaths, praying for an ending and his
freedom.
Then, silently, the beloved life force vanishes from his hands
we hold.
We are all suspended in his twenty-five.

Free At Last

In 1975, I brought him a Valentine card I had made, twenty-four little red hearts scattered, one for each year we had been married. He had been in the nursing home since early December, slowly losing to the two-year onslaught of his own rogue cells. His pain was barely controlled by the available medication.

His gift to me? His decision to stop taking nourishment, to bring it all to a close. He had considered his plan in the long quiet nights, and shared his reasons: to save the expense, to end the pain, and, more importantly, to shorten the family's anguish as we watched him diminish day by day. It was time, and he was ready. Our pastor supported us for the journey.

Kisses and tears. I didn't try to change his mind. We agreed on his choice. His doctor arranged for the food trays to stop, and, after a while, the saline IV.

After five weeks, on a cold March night, he left us, his plan realized. His sister and I felt his force leave the pale hands we held. We kissed his quiet cheek. The minister who was with us said a blessing. We stepped out into the crisp cold air. I looked up to a sky filled with stars.

Free at last.

Black Car

A late March evening, cold, new snow underfoot.
The funeral home had sent a car to take us to the church.
An immaculate long black sedan, probably a Cadillac or Lincoln.
The gloved driver held the door; we slid onto the wide leather back seat.
The motor purred; none of us had ever ridden in such luxury.

It was Wednesday, but we were dressed in Sunday clothes;
The widow, the daughter, the son.
A quiet ride, only four blocks, a few hushed words.
Then, too soon, we were at the church.

We emerged from the car's warm cocoon.
Waiting for us inside—psalms, prayers, a Bach fugue, hymns.
Tearful friends and family---hugs and offered comfort.
After, sharing coffee and cake and memories.
People doing their earnest best.

The black car took us home through icy streets;
A short trip to our new life—minus one.

Weathering the Storm

The storm blew and battered her,
Crushing her world.
After, she huddled in her empty cave,
Her center in shadows.

Then, slowly, soft voices filtered through.
Kind hands reached out, gently urging,
Nudging her back to the light, with love.

Two Thanksgivings

We always had golden glow salad on our Thanksgiving table. I used my mother's recipe of crushed pineapple, grated carrots, diced celery and orange gelatin, served in a cut glass bowl. That year, there were five of us around the table: my widowed sister-in-law Sarah, her son Steve from Boston, my son Mark and his wife Sandy, and myself. The bountiful serving dishes were in place, so many, in fact, that there was no room for the golden glow salad and Sandy's cranberry gelatin mold. These two dishes had been placed on a side tray table. The wine was poured and we were ready to eat.

Then I noticed that the candles were unlit. As Mark went to the sideboard drawer for matches (special small wooden ones in a fancy box that had belonged to my parents), he backed into the tray table, upsetting the quivery salads. Emergency! The cranberry mold luckily landed right side up, slightly askew, and we slid it back to the center of the plate. The golden glow was not so fortunate; it landed upside down, with about half of it oozing down into the metal grate of the floor heating register. The remainder clung to the unbroken glass bowl, so all was not lost.

Mark and Steve sprang into action, lifting the grate into a dishpan and scooping up the orange residue which, luckily, had not plummeted down into the hot air furnace. As the rest of the family at the table kept watch over the rapidly-cooling turkey and trimmings, they carried the whole mess to the kitchen, rinsed and dried the grate and rejoined us. Then, the candles finally glowing, we drank a toast and joined in a prayer of thanks for the food, for our family and, with smiles, for another small adventure to bind us together.

Now, another Thanksgiving, two years later. My sister-in-law Sarah had made reservations for us at a festive restaurant brunch in her small town. But, our plans had tragically changed, for Sarah had died in the hospital the night before Thanksgiving after an unexpected one-week illness. Her brother, Charles, from Florida and her son, Steve had come during her last days, and we gathered, bereft, in her home on the holiday morning. Anne was due to arrive the next day from Boulder to join Mark, Sandy and me.

We decided to go to the brunch, but, arriving at the scheduled time, found a note on the door saying that it had been canceled due to lack of other reservations. Sarah, of course, had not received notice. There were no other nearby restaurants open. We sat in the car in a state of limbo. No funeral plans could be made until Friday. A long sad day loomed.

We decided that we would cook a Thanksgiving dinner. Luckily, a small supermarket was still open. We swept in, the only customers, and gathered the ingredients we would need---a good-sized chunk of unsliced deli turkey breast, potatoes, squash, bread, celery and onions for the stuffing, cranberry sauce, salad greens, mushrooms for gravy, rolls and pumpkin and apple pies.

Returning to the echoing house, we opened a bottle of wine with an improvised corkscrew made of a nail and pliers. Steve and Sandy, both excellent cooks, went into action in the unfamiliar kitchen, a challenge. Mark and I washed the pots and pans as they stirred, cubed and whisked their way to an innovative yet traditional meal. Charles sat before the television in the living room, only partially aware of the football game through his grief over the realization that his last sibling was gone.

We found Sarah's lace tablecloth, good china and goblets, all of which had not been used since her husband's death. We lighted the candles, again remembering the golden glow episode.

At last we came to the table, having filled the long gray afternoon. We joined hands and said a prayer of thanks for those who were now separated from us, and for Sarah's life and all that she had meant to us. We asked for strength to face the difficult days ahead.

Then we ate our Thanksgiving dinner, surrounded with warmth and love.

Masked and Dangerous

It was a dark Saturday night in late October. This was back in the day when I was an antique dealer, and friends and I were displaying our wares at an annual show and sale. Eight of us were meeting for dinner at our favorite local restaurant at the end of a long day, but I told them I was too tired to join them. They went innocently on their way.

My Hallowe'en plan unfolded. I hurried home and turned myself into Nurse Priscilla: a white uniform with some extra bosom area padding, a clown wig topped with a crisp white cap, long white underwear, green Converse hi-top sneakers, rubber gloves and an opaque clown mask. I carried a shopping bag nursing kit, containing an out-sized wooden spoon tongue depressor and a red rubber hot water bottle with enema tube attached. A stethoscope dangled around my neck to complete the picture of pure professionalism. I climbed in my car and headed to the restaurant where my unsuspecting friends were relaxing, unaware that they were to be Nightingaled.

I bustled in and stopped at one or two booths, where I silently took pulses, nodded my head gravely and suggested an enema to the baffled but laughing diners.

I then headed to my friends' table where I offered my services to the wary group, boldly pulled up a chair and joined them, never speaking a word. Puzzled but polite, they offered to buy me a drink (they had had one or two while waiting for dinner to arrive). I accepted, but then the jig was up. There was no way I could drink while wearing my stiff plastic clown mask, so off it came My prank became famous in the local antique community.

An Election Experiment

It was November, 1980. I entered the village church polling place on a mission. I had previously noted that, when election results were printed in our weekly newspaper, there were never any write-in-votes recorded. It would seem that, over the years, some prankster would have voted for Mickey Mouse or Gregory Peck. So, I was going to do it.

It was five o'clock, and there were short lines as people stopped after work to vote for village mayor. The registering desk was staffed with the usual retired women (it may have been a lifetime appointment) who had been there since six that morning, with their homemade cookies and coffee, doing their governmental tasks. I stood in line in front of a nervous eighteen-year-old who was voting for the first time. I reassured him that it was a simple procedure.

Finally, my turn. I stepped into the voting booth, closed the curtain and opened the small sliding write-in door. There was no paper, and no writing tool. I poked my head out of the booth and called for help. One of the voting ladies scurried over and stepped inside with me to inspect the deficient apparatus. She went to the back of the machine and looked; the problem was beyond her training.

She conferred with the other women, and they decided that this emergency needed expert attention. Meanwhile, the anxious young voter waited for his turn.

This was before the days of cell phones, so the church office phone was used to call the village Election Inspector, David

Davis. Now, David was a large fiftyish local citizen, semi-employed, who basked in this important position. On election day, he had a flashing light on his Chevy station wagon as he roared up to the church.

"What's the matter here?" he asked loudly as he swept into the church hall. He ordered me out of the booth, made his inspection, removed a panel on the back and confirmed the absence of the materials necessary for a write-in vote. I was not able to vote at all since I had made the choice of writing in which locked me out of the regular levers.

Inspector Davis stomped out, muttering. I left, disenfranchised. The machine was reset. The young voter, who had waited patiently, finally did his patriotic duty.

It remains unknown whether there has ever been a write-in vote recorded in the village, or if anyone has noticed, or even cares.

Our Green Companion

When I was about eight, a friend gave me a small plant from Woolworth's 5 & 10 cent store (some of you may remember those stores?) It was a snake plant (sansevieria). I cared for it during my schooldays; it thrived, putting forth tall sharp spiky leaves. My mother grudgingly tended it when I went away to college.

As soon as I was married and had a home of my own, the plant came to live with us. Well, we moved twelve times in fourteen years, and it went with us, usually to a corner of the living room. When the big white pot was situated, then the new place felt like home. I subdivided it many times and shared shoots with friends.

In the summer, I carried it to the front porch and sunshine, and it unexpectedly bloomed with fragrant spikes of white blossoms. Our local weekly newspaper carried a photo of this uncommon event. The family was proud; we had a celebrity.

Then, one June night, it disappeared from the porch. The village police took a report, but said that there had been a large number of late night thefts, with missing greenery, antique crocks, baskets and other decorative items. The Giffords felt violated and saddened. Ah, but the culprits later were caught as they made another midnight snatch. Two women, with a garage full of purloined foliage, confessed.

I was thrilled when the police told me my plant had been found. I was summoned to the station to make an I.D. There it was, among tables full of similar victims., but it had to remain there for evidence; I reminded them to be sure to water it. Happy ending---a policeman delivered it to me several weeks later, and we greeted it with smiles and some fertilizer.

Ah, but further adventures awaited.

Ten years later, as I got ready to move to Boulder, I again subdivided the plant and shared the shoots with neighbors. My daughter, Anne, and I packed our familiar friend carefully in my car, along with other valuables, and headed west from upstate New York. Well, south of Cleveland, we totaled my Ford. We and the salvaged contents of the car spent two days with a college friend in Cincinnati, and arranged to fly home to Boulder. The snake plant had to be left behind; our friend took it to her synagogue. Anne and I separated several roots, wrapped them in wet paper towels and plastic for their flight to Denver in my carry-on luggage. Luckily, they survived the security inspection. Our family friend would survive in Boulder.

I immediately re-potted the shoots, and they slowly multiplied. After fourteen years, I again divided off a healthy plant for my son in Arizona. My plant is putting up new growth and will be inherited by my daughter or grandson someday. It has been a very present part of our family history. I can only hope that its next 82 years will be more tranquil.

I wonder why we never gave it a name?

Blue

I love all shades of blue.

Pale forget-me-nots
The deep juiciness of blueberries
The basic crispness of a navy dress
A cobalt glass vase be-jeweled by sunlight
The sapphire sparkle of my mother's ring
Blue gingham stars appliqued with love on great-
grandmother's quilt
The unique pulsating sky in a Maxfield Parrish painting
A glacier's icy blue
A peacock feather's azure iridescence
The shimmer of a mountain lake
A baby's eyes
Two aqua dresses: the one I wore to my husband's funeral,
and my dress at my son's garden wedding
And, finally, the unique deepness of a Colorado sky.

Birds I Have Known

I am afraid of birds. I don't know why. I enjoy watching them at a feeder, but I do not want to be in a situation where I might actually be touched by one. Here are two stories about Priscilla and birds.

Fifty-five years ago our family was visiting at my sister-in-law's farm home. The young children were playing inside, and I was helping hang new drapes in the living room. I was balanced on a small stepladder, trying to fasten the small hooks on the rod, when suddenly, a yellow parakeet swooped crazily around my head. My nephew had freed his pet bird, "Petie", from his cage, and the ecstatic bird began circling in my general area. I dropped the drapes, jumped off the ladder and ran into the nearby bathroom, slamming the door and screaming. The adults present knew of my phobia and quickly returned the briefly-free bird to his cage. My puzzled nephew asked, "Why is Aunt Priscilla screaming in the bathroom?" Why, indeed.

Twenty-five years ago, returning home from a long day away, I drove my car into the garage, walked toward my house and was horrified to find a pigeon on my small back porch, blocking my entrance to the house. I clapped my hands and shouted. The bird just hopped a bit; apparently it had a broken wing and could not fly away. An ordinary person simply would have stepped around him; not this person. My front screen door was latched from the inside, so I couldn't get into my house. What did I do? I went to my elderly housebound neighbor's and called the village police.

Within minutes, a young policeman arrived and walked up the driveway, his holstered pistol at the ready for any emergency.

"What seems to be the matter, ma'm?"

"There's a pigeon on my porch."

"I see."

"I'm afraid of birds. Could you move him out of the way?"

The uniformed cop mounted the three steps, poked at the bird and determined that, indeed, its wing was broken. Decision time. "I could call the animal control officer, but it's just a hurt pigeon. Is it all right if I just destroy it?"

"Yes, please," I answered in a shaky voice.

He asked me to fetch a plastic trash bag from the garage and took the bird and bag behind the building. I expected to hear a pistol shot, but he must have used some less violent means of dispatching the bird. He returned with the bag, the ex-bird inside, and put it inside the lidded trash can, after assuring me that the bag was fastened securely.

He got out his clipboard and took down my name, address and time of the incident. I noticed that he had a rather puzzled grin. His final words were, "I'm just wondering how to write this up." We laughed, I thanked him and he drove away in the squad car, ready for the next village emergency.

I wonder what he told his buddies back at the station.

First Kiss

This is not a story of pubescent romantic angst. It does not describe nervous shyness and colliding eyeglasses, or lips not quite on target; no sweaty palms dangling uncertainly.

No, this is a tale of a seven-month old baby boy discovering how to give a kiss.

My grandson had been blessed with countless kisses from his family. He had severe allergies, and much loving daily attention during his beginning months. On this spring day, he had just nursed to satisfaction. His mother handed him to me for a cuddle and a burping. He suddenly reared back from my shoulder, looked at me and sweetly attacked my cheek with an open-mouthed, sloppy application of his lips. Then he unat-tached, laughed and did it again. By this time, his mother and I were squealing in delight. I handed him to his mother, and he planted a few of his experimental smacks on her face. It was obviously a very pleasant first-time experience for him.

That day he discovered a a pleasant new way to be close to others. His kisses were quickly fine-tuned and less juicy.

Today he is twenty-nine, and every visit begins and ends with an "I love you" and a kiss. It is still sweet.

Curiosity

"Why?" asked the four-year old boy.

Let's start at the beginning.

It is a well-known anatomical fact that when women reach a certain age, the flesh on the underside of their upper arms loses its firmness. This is an understatement: it sags and flops around, and tightening the muscle does no good. There is no muscle involved. The superfluous skin just hangs there.

My grandson and I were riding in the back seat of the car on a summer day. I had on a sleeveless shirt, comfort having conquered vanity. He began playing with my mobile upper arms, which he had named "flabbage". He made the skin wobble from side to side, carefully studying the movement. He noted that his mom's arms were not like that, and asked why grandma's arms were so different.

With a hug, I answered, "God gave grandmas flabbage to amuse small boys on long car trips."

He soon tired of his amusement, and we began counting cows and horses in the fields.

Phantom Friend

They say when a limb is severed
You still feel its weight.
The phantom pain is real.
Your eyes tell you it is no longer there,
But the nerves somehow pulse on.
The loss is not yet final.

Death separated my friend from me.
I sense her still.
I think, "I'll call her."
I think, "I'll take her some raspberries."

My mind tells me she is gone.
In my heart, she still throbs on.

A Child's Birthday

The child was almost six, that magical age when the angel dust still clings. She and her sister were home-schooled; she read easily. Stories about fairies were her special favorites. Excited about her approaching January birthday, she loved to hear over and over the details of her birth—the time, her weight, what she looked like.

The night before her birthday, with her mother's puzzled help, she set her alarm clock for 3:15 in the morning. She would reveal only that it was a secret surprise and smiled herself to sleep.

At 3:30, she crept sobbing into her parents' bed. Quieted by their kisses, she tearfully revealed the reason for her anguish. The fairies had not come! She had read or been told that each year, on the hour of your birth, the fairies came and danced outside your window. Her alarm had awakened her, she had run to the window ready for magic, to see only the bare wintry garden glistening with snow. Nary a fairy.

Her folks suggested that fairies, being gauzy creatures, might not have parkas, mittens and boots. Perhaps it had been too cold for them. Somewhat consoled, the child cuddled between them and was soothed to sleep.

They awoke to her birthday. She was now officially six, and there were gifts, cake and love all around. But, at quiet times during the day, she thought about the fairies. She decided that perhaps they really had come and danced for her, but under orders from their queen, were not allowed to be seen. Next year, she would open the window to the cold night air and listen more carefully for tinkling bells, wee voices, or even laughter. (Based on a true story).

North Coast

We drive north past rows of fruit trees,
Orchards on each side of the two-lane road.
Trees loaded with green apples, patiently turning to September's juicy crimson.
We pass roadside stands: baskets of cherries, early peaches, sweet corn, green beans.
Full summer in upstate New York.

Then, we can drive no farther.
We are at the North Coast, the great Lake Ontario,
With Canada lying unseen miles over the water.

The old stone lighthouse marks the mouth of Sodus Bay.
We climb the steep metal stairs to the 150-year-old lens.
A museum now; the new automatic light on the pier does the warning work.
Sailboats slice through the dark choppy water.
A few fishermen bounce along in their motorboats.

Below, on the narrow beach, a man and boy are skipping stones.
The man's shale wafer bounces six times on the surface before sinking.
The boy's plunks to the bottom.
The man shows the boy how to pick the perfect thin stone.
He teaches him the correct grip; the sideways wrist action, the quick release.
The boy tries, and tries again, and finally, his stone hops and skims over the water.

We look down from the lighthouse. Thousands of boys and countless skipped stones over the years. All is well.

Wyoming Adventure

We had two choices when our rental compact Toyota bogged down in the Wyoming sand drift. We could wait and hope that help would come, or walk toward civilization.

First, some background. My daughter Anne, my twelve-year-old grandson Lex, and I were driving from Boulder to Jackson Hole where we would meet my son, Mark and his wife, Sandy, who had flown west from Rochester, NY. We planned to join together for a family week in Yellowstone.

We three had spent the night in Rock Springs, Wyoming. My AAA guidebook listed a nearby sand dune area, with petroglyphs and wild horses. It was on our route to Jackson Hole. Perfect. The young motel clerk provided directions, and we were off on a hot August Sunday morning. We easily found the turn-off road, and noted several trucks towing all-terrain vehicles; they veered off to an ATV riding range. Another small sign pointed to the sand dunes. We drove on happily, playing our Elvis tapes and searching for wild life. Ah, this was the real West.

Anne had driven about two miles when the narrow road became covered with sand. Just as we considered turning back, we became mired up to the hubcaps in a large sand drift. Having experience with upstate New York snow drifts, we tried rocking the small car back and forth, with no success. Rental cars do not come equipped with snow shovels; we had no digging tools. We were alone, with water, snack food and no cell phone. Mark and Sandy were waiting for us in Jackson

94

Hole. I envisioned hikers finding our bleached bones in this bleak desert.

After a few quietly frantic moments, (not wanting to alarm Lex), we made a plan. If another car didn't appear on the lonely road in ten minutes, Anne, who was in good shape from her Boulder swimming and hiking, would walk back to the ATV turn-off, hoping to flag down someone or call for assistance. We sat in the car, out of the blazing sun, while Lex stayed outside and spotted two antelopes. Silent prayers.

As Anne was assembling water for her hike, a cloud of dust appeared. A large 4WD pickup truck careeened toward our stalled car. It stopped, and a husky man and two teen-aged boys piled out. Their families had weekend-camped further ahead in the sand dune area described in our guidebook. Their return was delayed by mechanical trouble with another vehicle back at the campsite; they were headed back to Rock Springs to buy a truck part.

The timing was exquisite, as the road was very little traveled. The boys attached a chain, pulled our car free and turned it around. I wiped away my tears of relief as we chatted with our rescuer, and gratefully gave him $50. He explained that a road sign prohibiting small vehicles must have fallen down, and directed us to a safer exit.

He asked where we were from; we explained that we were from Boulder. Adjusting his Stetson, his parting words were, "We don't get many visitors in this part of Wyoming, and we like it that way."

Night Garden - A Poem for Glo

Note: My neighbor, forty-two, died at home of kidney disease
in November. Near the end of her struggle, late one night she
asked to be carried outside to see her beloved garden. Her
husband wrapped her warmly and carried her to the porch.
This poem was written on the morning of her death.

They helped me to my garden in the night.
The bedded borders waited for the cold that lurked,
 As always, just beyond November.

My grateful eyes revived the darkened husks,
And they rose young and green and sweet,
And it was Spring, as it shall be again.

Winter

This year it kept snowing and snowing
And the bitter wind never stopped blowing.
Although our poor noses
Grew red like the roses,
Now it's March, and a crocus is showing.

Spring Times Three

One year I was dazzled on my travels by three Springs.

One—San Francisco, Late February

A city in bloom.
Trees dressed in pink and white.
Shrubs bursting red and yellow.
Orderly tulips seen from the clanging, climbing cable car.
Primeval Muir redwoods rising from spongy fern-covered soil..
All of this nourished by gentle morning rain that baptized the
city.
Fierce torrents drenching the Chinese New Year crowds;
A polite sea of bright umbrellas waiting for the lion dancers.
Evening fog, the city's trademark.
And everywhere, surprising Spring.

Two—Boulder, Late March

Suddenly mild, the sun full of promises.
Brave purple, yellow and white crocus testing the air.
Pansy faces poking through stubborn snow patches.
Forsythia arching golden in garden corners.
Grass still brown, trees thinking about budding.
Cold winds still lurking,
But for today, a taste of Spring.

Three—Upstate New York, Early May

Rain, puddling everywhere.
Pussy willows gone to yellow fuzz.

Crocus, wilted, over and done.
In the orchards, acres of apple and cherry trees,
Their straight rows of blossoms promising fruit in its season.
In the back yard, violets and blue forget-me-nots,
Slender stalks of lily-of-the-valley bearing their sweet white cups.
And in the far back corner by the white fence
The old lilac bush, its branches heavy with perfumed purple.

Spring.

The Front Porch

Every May for forty years, I settled the front porch.

The gray-painted wooden floor was scrubbed with a sudsy broom, rinsing away the winter's grit. The green fiber rug was unrolled and spread. The bamboo blind was hung at the west end to block the late summer sun. The sturdy redwood settee, chairs and small tables were hauled from the garage to their summer homes. The green and brown slipcovered cushions were brought down from their dry winter attic storage. The wind chime, a ceramic barn with improbable dangling pigs, was hung. The pale houseplants were carried out for their sun-soaked summer vacation. Pots of red geraniums, coleus, blue lobelia and bright petunias were placed here and there on weathered apple crates. The flag flew from its holder. The porch was ready.

In the early days, the children spent hot afternoons playing Monopoly there with friends. My husband waited there after work, reading the paper, until supper was ready. Our teen children took over after dark. Later, it was a place for me to sit and read, to eat my solitary meals, to watch the neighborhood kids play, to wave to their parents, to serve a cold glass of iced tea to friends, and to watch the fireflies in the evening before the mosquitoes drove me indoors.

Now, our house and the porch have a new owner. The furnishings are dispersed. I have journeyed on, but I have a photo of that pleasant place on my refrigerator, helping me to remember.

Please Wait

It was 2::30 a.m. I was asleep. I was suddenly awakened by a female voice saying, "Please wait for the beep." It was the robotic yet melodic voice on my answering machine speaking to me. I was immediately at full attention. What did it mean? It must be very important to call in the middle of the night. Of course I would wait as directed.

I raced to the bathroom, carrying my portable phone with me so I would not miss the beep. Then, on the ready, I rummaged around the kitchen, ate a banana, then a popsicle, always on the beep alert.

After an anxious silent hour, l reluctantly crawled back into bed. Sleep never came, but neither did the promised beep. The alarm clock sounded at seven, and I moved into my day, foggy and unrested, still beepless.

It will remain one of those little happenings that lift our hum-drum lives into the realm of the mysterious.

Stuck, Again!

I sometimes need help getting out of a tight situation.

On my first kayaking experience with my family, I paddled around happily on a pond and headed toward the beach. My son pulled the craft up on the sandy shore, steadying it so I could get out. Problem: I could not get the leverage to emerge from that slim boat. I suggested that they strap me, inside the kayak, on top of the car. Finally, he and his sister extricated me. It has become a family fable.

Another time, the family and I were floating around in the Water World's Lazy River. I was splendidly sprawled in a large tube, wearing a white crew hat and tee shirt to ward off sunburn, my legs dangling over the side. My grandson delighted in steering me into the soaking fountains. The others tired of this tame fun and moved on to the Wave and Slide. I stayed behind, drifting aimlessly. When I tried to get out at the steps, my 79-year-old knees were too creaky. After several more wet circuits, an attendant (or maybe two), pried me out and I rejoined the family.

And then, there was the ferris wheel at the county fair. The ride chairs of my childhood were wooden with chains, but these modern ones were molded white plastic, with the seat only a foot off of the floor. That should have been a warning. Well, the night ride was exciting, with the fair's gaudy neon lights below us. When our car stopped, two kind women and my daughter had to come to my rescue and help me lurch out onto solid ground.

There's more.

Finally, we went to the Carousel of Happiness in Nederland, Colorado, a bright, restored ride with hand-carved animals. With minimal difficulty I climbed onto a large white and black cow. Round and round, humming and smiling along to the old music, then slowing to a stop. The cow had a large curled tail; I could not swing my leg over it to dismount. I finally succeeded with the help of two strong-armed attendants. We learned later that they re-designed the tail to accommodate older merry-go-round lovers. One of my friends had the same experience; we moo at each other when we meet.

Lately, my family supports me in my decision to play it safe.

Oh, well.

Jamaican Adventure

It was December 24. I was in Jamaica, and I needed to buy some underpants.

After many delays, canceled flights and a general holiday air travel nightmare, we had finally arrived in Negril for a Christmas week family vacation. However, my luggage was in Miami, promised to arrive in two or three days. My daughter, Anne, and I set out to buy some underwear to tide me over.

We hailed one of the numerous local taxis, negotiated a fare and went on a wild ride on the left side of the road into town, honking at pedestrians and chickens in the road. Stately native women balancing baskets of fruit or large cartons on their heads stepped gracefully out of our path.

We disembarked at a center of small shops selling souvenir items, jewelry, wood carvings, and knit rasta hats and tee shirts in the red, yellow and green national colors. We stopped in a small supermarket which offered snack foods, rum, many flavors of condensed milk, 25-pound sacks of rice and beans, coffee, grocery staples, disposable diapers and a long really baffling shelf of 6-ounce bottles of food coloring. All this, but no undies.

We entered a small clothing store which featured sneakers, glittery platform sandals, bright ruffled taffeta dresses and Spandex everything. The underwear line in the glass case consisted of minuscule thongs, bikinis, boy-cut panties with cowboy nailhead trim and similar garments. The young male clerk shook his head at our request, "Sorry, mama."

The Jamaicans are very considerate of old folks, I was always addressed as "mama", a contrast to the usual "Hey, mon!" greeting.

Our taxi driver had explained, "They took care of us; now we will take care of them." We saw very few older natives, and I learned later that the life expectancy of someone born in 1950 is only 57 years on that third-world island.

Anyway, back to our search. In another shop, we found a pair of orange nylon briefs with multicolored stripes. The helpful clerk assured us that they would fit me. Marked size XXL, they seemed a skimpy far cry from my usual cotton Fruit of the Looms, but it was 90 degrees and we were weary. We bought them. After lapping up mango and papaya ice cream cones, we hailed a cab back to the hotel.

As I was experiencing the secret thrill of my Jamaican undies the next day, my luggage arrived. I do wonder, though, what Jamaican grandmas wear. Perhaps they are only in their forties and wear thongs, directly going to Depends as needed.

Procrastination

P---Perhaps tomorrow

R---Really, I'm thinking about it

O---Only a few more preparations needed

C---Can you explain it to me just once more?

R---Readying my materials

A—After I finish what I'm doing now

S —-Still thinking about it

T—-Trying to get enthusiastic

I —-Inspiration is slowly forming

N—-Not quite ready, though

A—-Almost time to start

T—-Trying to find the energy

I—- I'm really thinking about it now

O—- Organizing my thoughts

N—- NOW!!

In the Middle of the Night

The windows here at Golden West senior community are never dark. One might think that a few hundred elders living in a high-rise would turn out the lights and settle down in their apartments at a reasonable hour. Some do, but not all. Standing outside on the sidewalk during the middle of the night, one can see lighted windows scattered across the building's facade.

Whatever are folks doing?

Watching television movies and infomercials.
Shopping on QVC.
Eating a bag of potato chips.
Doing the daily newspaper crossword, Sudoku or cryptogram puzzles.

Making a trip to the bathroom.

Having a cup of cocoa and some graham crackers.
Doing a load of laundry.
Taking that empty wine bottle to the recycle room on the next floor.
Balancing the checkbook.
Reading the Bible.

Making a trip to the bathroom.

Googling a high school friend on the computer.
Playing solitaire on the laptop.
Looking through a daughter's wedding album.

106

Watching re-runs of "Everyone Loves Raymond", or "The Golden Girls".
Reading a book or a magazine.

Making a trip to the bathroom.

Doing yoga.
Remembering a July, 1985 family road trip.
Trying to remember yesterday's dinner.
Knitting or crocheting a sweater for a new grandbaby.

Making a trip to the bathroom.

And it's not necessarily sleepily silent, either. There are sounds.

The elevator doors open and close, open and close. Who are these nocturnal wanderers? Where are they going, where have they been? Are they in their pajamas?

The huge food delivery truck backs into the loading dock, beeping. When the windows are open in the summer, the driver's radio music drifts upward.

A toilet flushes.

Tidy nocturnal neighbors slam the trash chute door.
A shower runs, and runs, and runs.
Hall doors bang shut as the paper person arrives to deliver the morning news.
A siren is quieted as the firetruck and emergency vehicle approach the building, summoned to help one of us in distress.

A toilet flushes.

A neighbor's TV is tuned to an Australian soccer game.
The students across the road party on--- men getting louder,
women laughing shrilly until all the car doors slam and they
move on, tires squealing, to another social location.
A pet dog down the hall barks once or twice until hushed.

A toilet flushes.

In the middle of the night.

The New Year

The new year comes.

I take down the old calendar
With its cavorting cats.
The daily squares are reminders
Of how I filled the year, one day at a time.

I hang the new calendar on its kitchen nail.
A photo of ripe tomatoes greets me on the page.
The empty squares await.

There.

Ready, set, live.

Resolutions

In this new year, we resolve

To do more of this, less of that;

To try something new, bury our failures.

A secular Lent
And, perhaps for some, an alleluia.

Letter from my Hands

Dear Priscilla,

Well, we've been together for a long time. Years ago, we were both small. We instinctively curled around the large fingers of your parents, who had waited seven long years for your arrival. Later, we touched their loving faces. You sucked on our fingers, which was fine until you got some teeth. We reached for your toes and your toys and for grandma's eyeglasses. You learned that we could help you reach all sorts of places. We pulled you up to wobble from chair to couch, and then your folks held us as you tottered along, learning to walk.

Year by year, we helped you to independence. We put food in your mouth and all around it. We finally learned to tie your shoes and buttoned your sweater. We buckled your galoshes in the winter. We mastered the toothbrush. We wiped your bottom.

Lefty liked to fill in the pictures in your coloring books with waxy crayons, and then to write letters with a stubby pencil on lined paper. Lefty learned to cut out paper dolls with blunt-end scissors, to embroider with yarn on punched cardboard, and to string wooden beads on a cord.

We don't believe you thought of us very often, but we were always there; learning to crochet, to iron handkerchiefs, to use your Girl Scout knife (we still have a scar), to throw a ball, to bait a fishhook in the boat with daddy, to learn to row on the lake, to lace up your ice skates, to tighten the clunky roller skates, to play marbles and jacks, to hold the red wooden handles of the jump rope, to make a snowball and to hang on to the rubber handle grips of your bike.

We put pin curls in your hair, and Tangee lipstick on your lips, and fastened your first stockings to your garter belt. Then, when there were no more stockings during World War II, we spread leg makeup on your still-skinny legs, drawing a fake seam up the back with eyebrow pencil. You kept us clean but you didn't fuss over us. No nail polish. Some lotion. A signet ring.

We learned to type, a skill that we still use on the computer every day.

The years went by. A diamond and a gold wedding ring were added. We helped you share pleasure in your marriage. Caring for your babies introduced us to the sweet and the unpleasant tasks, but we were there--bandaging, bathing, smoothing ruffled hair and feelings. We plunged into the garden soil. In the kitchen, we kneaded, stirred, whisked, blended, measured, baked and sliced. We scrubbed and swept and dusted, cut and sewed, washed and ironed. We held the steering wheel and washed the car.

Later, we had to learn nursing skills: to give injections and bed baths and comfort for the sad years.

Now, we are veiny and wrinkled, stiff fingers veering off in arthritic directions---but still a part of you, still doing what we can to keep us steady on our journey.

Love, Your hands

FINALLY

Lessons Learned

Never write an anonymous letter; it can leave collateral damage.

When I was young, it was good to be an only child, but, now that I am old, I wish there had been a sibling with whom I could share memories.

Smile often, privately and publicly.

To cover up a scratch on furniture, rub your finger along your nose and apply the absorbed oil on the scratch.

Look for some good in every situation, sometimes barely discernible, but still a glimmer of grace.

It is hard to get out of a kayak if your knees don't work.

If you live long enough and listen, you'll finally find out about your kids' exploits as they grew up.

There is healing comfort in music.

Carry a small flashlight and a Swiss army knife in your purse.
.
When you hear an ambulance or fire truck siren, say a little prayer for the helpers and the helped.

As you learn of the death of old friends, be thankful for their long lives and grateful for the years that may remain for you.

People like to be called by their names.

To bear a grudge only hurts and sours yourself; the offender probably doesn't care or remember; he has moved on.

"Please" and "Thank You" are the grease of human interaction.

Others don't pay as much attention to how you look as you think they do. Relax.

Play the "granny card"---when people step forth to help you or offer a benefit because of your age, accept it with a smile. You're entitled.

When traveling, never pass up a chance to sit down or to use a bathroom. Always take time to eat when you are hungry; otherwise, everyone gets cranky and the museum is no fun. Always travel with a St. Christopher medal in your purse.

Saved popsicle sticks make great plant cultivation tools, and are also efficient scrapers to remove dog poop from shoe treads.

Always stop to soak up a sunrise, a sunset, a thunderstorm, a rainbow—all of them gifts. Then say "Thanks".

Love your family, warts and all, and tell them so often.

Evolution of Dreams

Baby—food, warmth, comfort, love

Childhood—princess, superhero, sports star

Young adult---college, career, relationships

Adult---family, stability, community

Retired---travel, health, security, exploration

Old age---food, warmth, comfort, love

Letter to My Feet

Dear Feet,

I must confess, I don't think about you very often unless an in-grown toenail throbs. You've been good pals down there for a long time. Let's remember all the shoes over the many years:

Dainty silk slippers for our baptism
Pink booties knitted with love and promptly kicked off
Laced toddler shoes for wobbly first steps
Red leather rubber-soled sandals for summer play
White rubber bathing slippers to protect you from the stony lake bottom
Shiny black tap shoes for attempted dancing
Many pairs of brown Girl Scout oxfords to fit your narrow width
Our first brown pumps—a one-inch high step into woman-hood
Red and white spectator heels the summer I was 20 and in love
White linen pumps to float us down the wedding aisle
Canvas Keds that I couldn't even see down there below my eighth-month belly
Sturdy shoes for support and comfort during the working years
And now, sensible sturdy flat shoes to carry us the rest of the way.

It has been a safe journey, except for the time in my eighties when I was dancing in the theater aisle, tripped and broke some of your bones. Sorry about that.

Thanks for the great ride.

Love, Me

The Christmas Letter

Fifty-five years of letters at Christmas.

Friends of our early married years, beginners, learning to be
parents.
We moved, they moved, finally to Colorado and North Caroli-
na,
But still the annual connection.
Job changes, kids' colleges and careers,
Weddings, grandchildren, vacations, trips---
All compacted in the holiday page, highlighting the positives.
Then, widowed, but still busy,
Trying to stay worthwhile.

And now this year, just this:
"I've moved to senior living and like it very much."

Good for you, Dottie.

Me, too.

Transition

All she is, quiet now.
Touch her, gently speak her name.
Whisper, "You may go."

My Vision

My eyesight was never a concern.

My first eyeglasses in seventh grade
Constant reading in high school
Unending books and papers in college
Then, finally time for novels and magazines,
Newspapers for the news and puzzles
Pleasure

Then, for motherhood, necessity:
Thumbing daily through Dr. Spock's fifties' baby Bible
Deciphering directions on the cake mix box
Locating a sliver in a small finger
Reading storybooks until they were seared in memory---
(Pokey Puppy ,Wyatt Earp, assorted bears, wolves, hens)
Threading the needle to stitch clothing and drapes
Darning socks and patching jean knees
Measuring sweet red cough syrup

Later, sight sometimes clouded by tears---
Recitals, graduations, weddings,
Being lost in a baby's wide gaze.
Funerals

Now, my vision and I are fading.
Large print, clunky telephone,
Talking books around the corner.

From here on, patient accommodation.

It Will Still Be Spring

When I can no longer see, I will still know when Spring arrives.

The birds, silent all winter, will sing me awake.
My head will be warmed by pure sunshine, freed from winter's cold.
The breeze, no longer chilled by snow, will kiss me gently.
My fingers will stroke the pussy willows' soft grayness.
The whir of the lawn mower will unlock the eternal sweetness of new grass.
The fresh rain will baptize my winter-stifled soul.
The unseen joy of Spring will enfold me once again.

I will celebrate with butter-dredged asparagus, and pungent chives, and rhubarb pie.

Celebration of Life

In the senior community, it's all there as we gather to remember her.

The guest book, the basket for condolence cards, vases of flowers on scattered tables.

Open photo albums---black and white snapshots, then some in almost-true color. There she is, a baby with proud parents, playing in the sand, a serious school picture, in cap and gown, laughing on a car's running board, a formal portrait of the whole strangely-serious wedding party. Then her children, followed by grandma holding the next generation. Retirement scenes---fishing trips, foreign cities, national parks. A life spelled out on glossy paper squares.

Sometimes there is a scrolling video of still shots or old home movies, produced for the occasion by a tech-smart grandchild.

And food, simple or elegant, to give us something to do as we visit and mingle with the others who have come to remember and to meet her family, perhaps for the first time. A bowl of red punch, or perhaps wine, maybe her favorite cookies.

A few words of tribute, a poem found in her Bible, some remembrances from family and old friends.

In an hour or two, we learn about this woman with whom we had shared our days in our retirement community.

At meals, we had come to know something about each other. A few questions and answers about a former life. Hometown tales. Stories of the accomplishments of children and grandchildren.
Snippets of her years, but now we see her complete.

How bittersweet that we knew so little when she was with us.

It might have been richer..

Mortality

The ketchup bottle is stamped, "Best used by April, 2019".
My credit card expires in February, 2020.
My passport was valid until November, 2016.

I wonder, "What is my expiration date?"
Could there be an invisible number, perhaps behind my right ear,
A marker of my mortality?
And would this be a firm date, a strict finality?
Or might it be just a suggested time,
Allowing me to risk limping on uncertainly, for a few more months or years?

I prefer not to know.

Ready

I am a dried husk
Waiting to be blown away.
Where is that sweet wind?

Old Lady

Remarked an old lady named Jenny,
Who lived with her cat in Kilkenny,
"Now birthdays are fine---
I'm happy with mine,
But I never expected so many!"

About the Author

Priscilla Gifford has been a reader and a writer for most of her almost-ninety years. She was born in upstate Auburn, NY, and received a B.A. in Sociology at Syracuse University. Married soon afterward to Paul Gifford, a medical technology manager, they eventually moved to Newark, NY, where they raised two children: Anne, a Boulder watercolor artist, and Mark (Sandy), a retired sound engineer in Sedona, AZ. Widowed in 1975, she was a nursing home social worker until retiring in 1989. She was also an antique dealer, a member of local historical societies, her church, and village organizations. She was an occasional traveler.

In 2002, Priscilla moved to Boulder to be near her daughter and grandson, Lexis. She plunged into her new life at Golden West Manor senior community, enjoying new friends, Scrabble, fitness, her computer and other activities. Many of the pieces in this book were composed in the Writing Group. Her musical interests include singing in the choir at Cairn Christian Church in Lafayette and playing jazz kazoo. In 2013, she and her daughter published a children's book, "Spike the Dhog".

Priscilla is tasting and enjoying the rich culture of Boulder.

Made in the USA
Middletown, DE
24 March 2019